BRITAIN'S
WORST WALKS

Travels around the UK's gloriously grim backwaters

Ben Hind

BRITAIN'S WORST WALKS

Summersdale Publishers Ltd
46 West Street
Chichester
West Sussex
PO19 1RP
UK

www.summersdale.com

Printed and bound in China

ISBN: 978-1-84953-455-0

Substantial discounts on bulk quantities of Summersdale books are available to corporations, professional associations and other organisations. For details contact Nicky Douglas by telephone: +44 (0) 1243 756902, fax: +44 (0) 1243 786300 or email: nicky@summersdale.com.

Photo Credits ©: Holmfirth 1 – Tim Green aka Atoach, Blackpool 2 – Matthew Wilkinson, Sellafield 1&2 – Gordon Edgar, Glasgow 1 – Matthew Wilkinson, Glasgow 2 – Graeme Maclean, Skegness 1 – Sam Stockman, City of London 1 – Dunc(an)

Contents

Introduction

Britain is a fantastic place for a walk. From snow-capped Highland peaks to the chalk cliffs towering over the English Channel; from moorlands where curlews call to the smoking factory chimneys that drove the Industrial Revolution; from the historic streets of our great cities to bucolic countryside that has been described as both green and pleasant, there are thousands of nice places to explore.

But few would disagree that some parts of our island are just a little bit... well, shit. That's not to say these places aren't worth seeing, of course, and here we come to the main objective of this book. In order to celebrate the rubbish bits of Britain, I give you the 13 most boring, pointless, unpleasant, dangerous, smelly and downright bloody awful walking routes in the whole of the country, along with tips for making them truly unforgettable.

For everyone who enjoys being outdoors, I hope this will provide a fresh and exciting challenge. Each walk can be achieved within a day or the whole sordid mess can be completed within one glorious fortnight. Why 13 walks? Well, put it this way, you must be pretty unlucky if this is how you end up spending your summer holidays.

Alternatively, you can sit at home and snigger at the fact that some idiot (i.e. me) actually decided to travel the length and breadth of the country researching them. But, however you want to savour the nation's worst walks, I can guarantee you will never look at Britain the same way again.

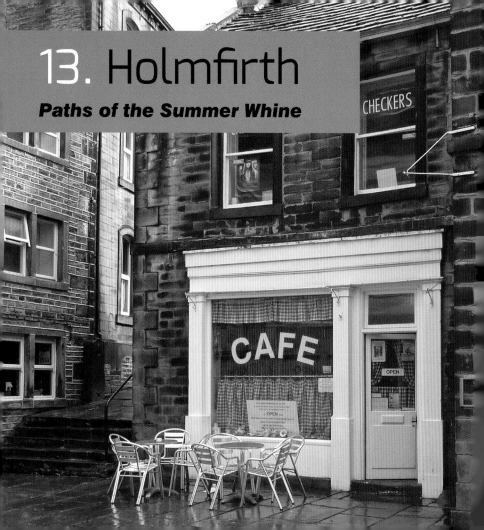

13. Holmfirth

Paths of the Summer Whine

Picturesque Holmfirth is a popular refuge for people who are happy to work in the nearby cities but would rather sell their firstborn into slavery than actually live there. However, this is not its only claim to infamy. *Last of the Summer Wine* was filmed hereabouts for 37 years, transforming the area into one of the biggest tourist attractions in Yorkshire. Due to the sitcom's growing popularity in the States, you will probably bump into some Americans – although be warned that many US viewers believe it to be a documentary. So, just when you thought you'd heard the last of the summer whine, for you, it's just about to begin...

- **Difficulty** – *Hip replacement*
- **Useful items** – *Wellies, woolly hat, bus pass, ferrets down your chuffin' trousers*
- **Likelihood of getting an erection at the thought of a mature lady in wrinkled nylons** – *Fair to middlin'*

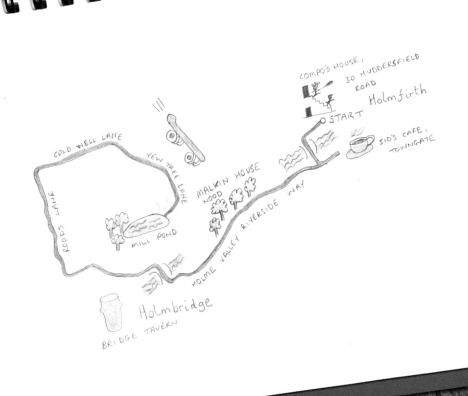

COMPO'S HOUSE, 30 HUDDERSFIELD ROAD

Holmfirth

START

SID'S CAFE, TOWNGATE

COLD WELL LANE

YEW TREE LANE

ROODS LANE

MALKIN HOUSE WOOD

MILL POND

HOLME VALLEY RIVERSIDE WAY

Holmbridge

BRIDGE TAVERN

1. Start at 30 Huddersfield Road, a museum located in the 'homes' of two fictitious TV characters – Bill 'Compo' Simmonite and Nora Batty. For anybody lucky enough to have never seen *Last of the Summer Wine*, Compo was a degenerate, tramp-like character who lived below the stone stairs, while Batty was his sour-faced upper neighbour who would often beat visitors with a broom. Compo was fixated by her wrinkled stockings and would in reality have belonged on some kind of offenders' register.

2. Cross the River Holme by the bridge on Victoria Street and arrive at Sid's Café on Towngate. This no-nonsense establishment, where the menu helpfully explains that a latte is a 'milky coffee', was a regular filming location for the show. It was where Compo, his timid pal Norman 'Cleggy' Clegg and the other one (the third character changed several times, although the longest serving was curmudgeonly 'Foggy' Dewhurst) would plot their ludicrous adventures over tea and insults. Go in for a cuppa and slurp it out of a saucer.

3. Leave Holmfirth along the Holme Valley Riverside Way footpath, which snakes through Malkin House Woods and takes you deeper into the fabulous Pennine scenery. Unfortunately, the stunning views are likely to be spoiled by memories of old men in unlikely situations, which will rise unbidden into your mind like phantoms and ruin any chance of a relaxing walk. There is no use fighting it, you can only give in. Therefore, after a pint at The Bridge Tavern at Holmbridge, you should proceed to the top of nearby Roods Lane. You will require a skateboard, a crash helmet, knee and elbow pads worn over ill-fitting tweeds and some kind of novelty device – for example, a wind turbine strapped to your back in the mistaken belief that it will generate enough electricity to supercharge your pacemaker. Skate as far as you can down Flush House Lane before careering off through the fields.

4. Two friends – one a peroxide blonde in a micro-dress and the other a terrified, weasel-like adulterer – should be holding a completely illogical romantic rendezvous up a tree somewhere near Cold House Lane. When you see their ladder, skate directly towards it, windmilling your arms and yelling like a maniac, and knock it to the ground, leaving the amorous couple unable to climb down from the boughs.

5. Continue on your skateboard down Yew Tree Lane until you meet a tractor pulling a load of manure. Luckily, there will be a sharp 180-degree turn that allows you to escape from the tractor's path – only to splash harmlessly yet hilariously into a mill pond. Stand up in the shallow, icy water and splutter angrily, glaring out from underneath the brim of your sodden woollen hat, as though your foolish behaviour was in fact somebody else's fault. Your walking companions should now make a whimsical comment, such as, 'That's dampened down his enthusiasm.'

6. Walk at least 12 miles in any direction and sit on a sunny hilltop, preferably one with soothing, bucolic views, in order to indulge in reflective, 'it's all for the best, I suppose' type speculation while chewing on a stalk of grass and contemplating that the walks can only go downhill from here.

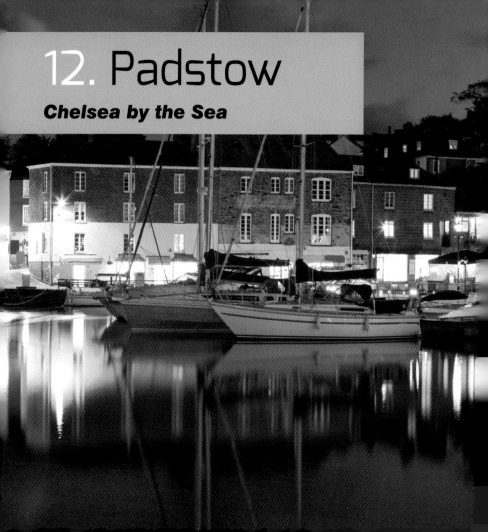

12. Padstow

Chelsea by the Sea

Padstow and Rock are the least affordable places to live in Cornwall, which is the least affordable place to live in Britain. For this rather sorry state of affairs, locals can thank the self-important tosspots who mill around these otherwise attractive seaside settlements. In order to blend in during this walk, you should loosely knot a pastel pullover around your shoulders, don a pair of absurdly expensive sunglasses and act as though the world owes you an incredibly good living, for no discernible reason other than you were born into a Sloaney family in London or the Home Counties.

- **Difficulty** – *Like spreading cold, hard butter on a crumbling scone*
- **Useful items** – *A working knowledge of Cornish insults (for instance, 'amm dhe'm gwenn, toll-din' means 'kiss my butt, arsehole', although most posh visitors think it means 'welcome to my wonderful county')*
- **Likelihood of bumping into your old cellmate from Strangeways** – *Minimal*

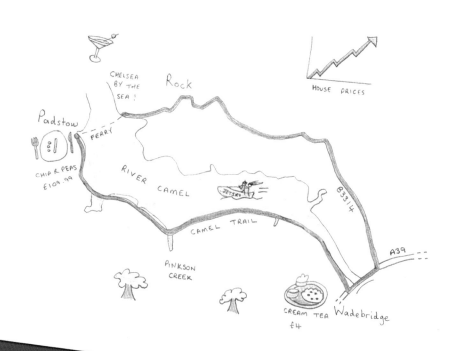

CHELSEA
BY THE
SEA!

Rock

Padstow

FERRY

HOUSE PRICES

CHIP & PEAS
£109.99

RIVER CAMEL

JETSKI

B3314

CAMEL TRAIL

A39

PINKSON
CREEK

CREAM TEA
£4

Wadebridge

1. Park somewhere in Padstow (which will cost roughly the same as actually buying a new car in some parts of the country) and walk down through the old fishing port to the harbour. If you are here in the summer, it will be bustling and busy – with crowds of stinkingly rich people who think that David and Samantha Cameron, who also holiday in the area, are just that little bit, ahem, middle class.

2. Walk to the harbour, passing one of seafood chef Rick Stein's four local restaurants. There are now two Michelin-starred places in tiny Padstow – compared to Glasgow, Manchester or Cardiff, for instance, which have none. However, the cost of eating out has increased markedly and fish suppers for all the family could set you back as much as would an hour of no-holds-barred kinkiness with a Belgravia prostitute. Furthermore, if you ask for a battered sausage with mushy peas (in the chippy, not in Belgravia), you will probably have a Jamie Oliver soufflé dish thrown at you as you are chased down a quaint, whitewashed back alley. Get out of Padstow as soon as is humanly possible by taking the foot ferry to Rock.

3. This is a charming, unspoilt quarry village, the polar opposite of the decadent dog-hole across the Camel... Ha! Of course not, or this would hardly be one of Britain's Worst Walks. Rock is even posher and more obnoxious than Padstow, if such a thing were possible. Even the wealthy summer residents of Padstow laugh at people in Rock because of their astronomically ridiculous sense of entitlement. Walk up Rock Road, past the sailing club and into the heart of the village known as 'Chelsea by the Sea'. If you feel the urge to vomit, just go with it – preferably into the back seat of a convertible Mercedes-Benz.

4. Rock has retained none of the charm and friendliness of its original inhabitants, and visitors wearing an inferior brand of polo shirt can expect to receive a welcome akin to a dead canary down a tin mine. There are more millionaires per head here than anywhere else in Cornwall, so at least you can be assured that the well-groomed strangers who sneer at you in the street and treat you with the respect normally reserved for the people who appear on *The Jeremy Kyle Show* or *My Big Fat Gypsy Wedding* are considerably richer than you are.

5. Turn inland at Shores Lane and head through the rolling countryside towards Little Dinham. Join the B3314 and walk to Wadebridge, a historic crossing over the River Camel. Follow the Camel Trail, a walking path built on the old railway line along the southern bank of the estuary, all the way back to Padstow. Look out for birds on the mudflats, such as cormorants, herons and terns, as well as braying boaters, yachties and waterskiers as the channel widens as it approaches the sea. Note: if you are shat on by one of the birds, you now know how young Cornish couples feel when all the local starter homes are bought up for a small fortune by people who will only use them three times a year.

6. As you get nearer to Padstow, look out for any other walkers who are out and about enjoying a stroll. This might be Cornwall but people around here bear little relation to the cider-swilling West Country stereotype. To test this theory, loudly hum a few bars of 'I've Got a Brand New Combine Harvester' as you approach them... and I bet they don't join in.

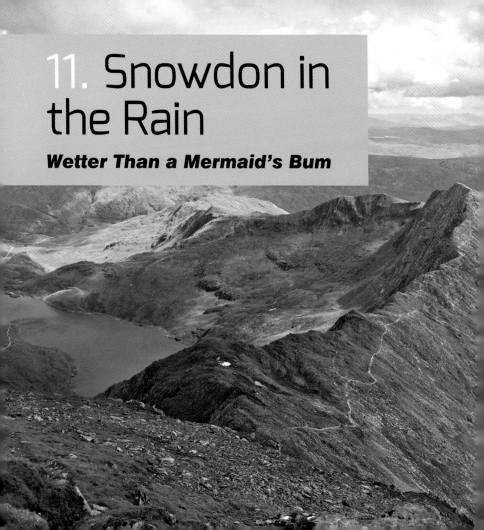

11. Snowdon in the Rain

Wetter Than a Mermaid's Bum

The name Snowdon comes from the Old English *snow dun*, meaning 'snow hill', but those Anglo Saxons were a rum lot – maybe they just wanted to encourage the early ski-holiday trade – because there is one type of weather that is much more common on Snowdon than snow, and that's rain. It rains here, a lot. Emrys G. Bowen, in his 1957 textbook *Wales: A Physical, Historical and Regional Geography* (it's a bit like *Fifty Shades of Grey*, only with less bondage... and more geography) states that Snowdonia gets more than 200 inches of rain every year. In other words, at 16 feet, 8 inches – or just over 5 metres – that's enough water to drown the average female giraffe.

- **Difficulty** *– Like swimming up a mountain*
- **Useful items** *– Cagoule, compass, Kendal mint cake, snorkel, flippers*
- **Likelihood of actually being able to see all five kingdoms from the summit** *– More chance of seeing Lord Lucan ride past on Shergar*

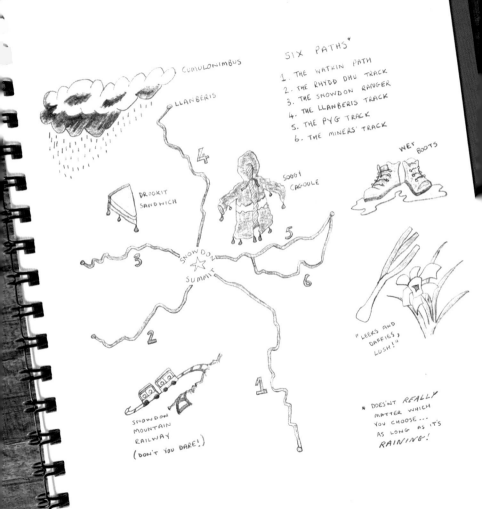

SIX PATHS*

1. THE WATKIN PATH
2. THE RHYDD DHU TRACK
3. THE SNOWDON RANGER
4. THE LLANBERIS TRACK
5. THE PYG TRACK
6. THE MINERS' TRACK

CUMULONIMBUS

LLANBERIS

DROOKIT SANDWICH

SOGGY CAGOULE

WET BOOTS

SNOWDON SUMMIT

"LEEKS AND DAFFIES, LUSH!"

SNOWDON MOUNTAIN RAILWAY (DON'T YOU DARE!)

* DOESN'T REALLY MATTER WHICH YOU CHOOSE... AS LONG AS IT'S RAINING!

1.   There are six main routes up Snowdon, and the longest slog is the Watkin Path, which was conceived by Lancastrian railway entrepreneur Sir Edward Watkin and opened in 1892. Park at the Hafod y Llan campsite on the southern flanks of the mountain, just off the A498; ideally, it should already be raining heavily as you get out of the car.

2.   Crib Goch, the knife-edge arête leading up to the summit (it is located to your north, somewhere within that huge and threatening grey cloud), is officially the wettest place in the United Kingdom. As you trudge up the hill towards it, you will already be starting to slither and slide in the mud. On average, most people climbing Snowdon in the rain will slip on their arse about five times (that stat wasn't from Emrys G. Bowen, by the way, I just made it up).

3. The wettest place on earth is Cherrapunji, in India, which receives 498 inches of rain a year on average. Other particularly soggy areas include such dream holiday destinations as Hawaii and Queensland and, according to old Emrys, the upper slopes of Snowdon would probably place just inside the global top 20; but without the tropical flip side of glorious, sizzling sunshine to dry your clothes between downpours. As you climb the path, it will feel like you are walking through God's endless and freezing cold shower.

4. There are lots of songs about rain that you can hum to keep your spirits up, such as 'The Pina Colada Song'. American singer-songwriter Rupert Holmes, who had a US number one with this irritating ditty in 1979, was actually born in Northwich, just across the border in Cheshire. He was the son of a US Army warrant officer and the family moved to New York when he was six, so he presumably never spent six hours being lashed by sheets of icy water while walking up a hill. No true Briton would equate getting caught in the rain with anything remotely pleasurable. (This relentlessly upbeat American attitude to precipitation is most famously illustrated by Gene Kelly in *Singin' in the Rain*; you've probably noticed that very few people tap dance in puddles on this side of the pond.)

5. They say that from the summit of Snowdon, you can glimpse all five kingdoms – England, Ireland, Scotland, Wales and Heaven. Unfortunately, in this kind of weather you are unlikely to see far beyond the torrent of water dripping from the hood of your cagoule. At 1,085 metres, Snowdon is no easy climb and you will soon feel like sitting down for a rest. However, the frigid rainwater trickling into your underwear will ensure that you don't sit down for long.

6. Keep going, up and up and up, into the clouds. Your feet will feel like blocks of ice; your skin will be chafing from the wet material and your red, raw fingers will be as nimble as a pack of pork sausages. Welcome to the wonderful world of hillwalking.

7.   There is a cafe on the summit of Snowdon, which was once famously described by Prince Charles as 'the highest slum in Britain'. Luckily for you, it has been renovated and is now rather nice. Unluckily for you, it does not always open in bad weather and is shut throughout the winter. In all probability, as you stagger into view, the staff will just be flipping the sign on the door over from *'agor'* (open) to *'ar gau'* (closed).

8.   There is nothing else for it but to turn around and begin your soggy descent. At least when you finally get back to the car and drop into a traditional Snowdonia pub to dry out before a roaring fire, you can expect a warm welcome from the locals (note – this does not apply if you are English).

10. Southend-on-Sea

End of the Pier Show

Imagine the following conversation, taking place between a father and his child over breakfast on a fine and bracing British Sunday morn.

Dad: 'Did you know that Southend Pier is the world's longest pleasure pier?'

Son: 'Go on, you're pulling my leg.'

Dad: 'It's true, junior. Longest pleasure pier in the whole wide world.'

Son: 'Wow! Can we go today, Dad?'

Dad: 'No chance. I'm off to the pub to watch the football, you can stay in and play on your Nintendo like you always do.'

- **Length** – 2.66 miles or 5.32 miles
- **Difficulty** – Easy
- **Useful items** – A pair of shoes, a candyfloss on a stick... that's about it
- **Likelihood of witnessing a pod of dolphins frolicking in the Thames** – You're 'avin' a larf, ain'tcha, you mug

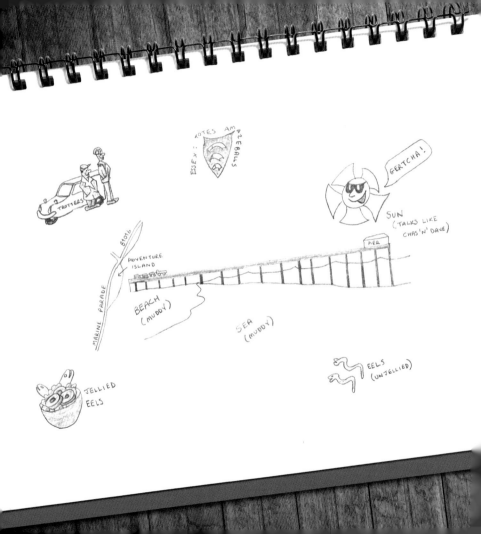

1. Start at Pier Hill, a refurbished area linking Southend High Street to the seafront. The art deco stylings, public artworks and cafe-culture vibe cost the taxpayer a cool £3.7 million, via the office of the deputy prime minister. So that's what he does.

2. Go over the Pier Bridge, pass through the Adventure Island funfair, walk around the lifeboat station and museum and arrive at the pier itself. At 1.33 miles in length, the pier you are now looking at is the longest pleasure pier... on... the... planet. Try not to faint from sheer excitement.

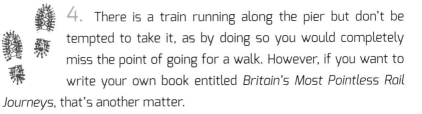

3. Begin walking along the wooden planks of the pier, across the vast mudflats and out towards the distant sea (where the water will have the same depressing brown hue as the contents of a motorway service station deep fat fryer). Breathe in the cold, ozone-fuelled air. Bask in the watery, pathetic sun. Try not to keep looking at your watch. Remember that Sir John Betjeman once said: 'Southend is the pier, and the pier is Southend.' Yes, I prefer the one he did about Slough, too.

4. There is a train running along the pier but don't be tempted to take it, as by doing so you would completely miss the point of going for a walk. However, if you want to write your own book entitled *Britain's Most Pointless Rail Journeys*, that's another matter.

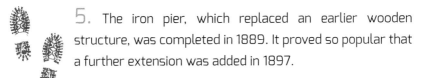

5. The iron pier, which replaced an earlier wooden structure, was completed in 1889. It proved so popular that a further extension was added in 1897.

6. As you stroll along, you might find it interesting to consider that Southport, Walton-on-the-Naze, Ryde, Llandudno, Ramsey, Hythe, Brighton, Bangor and Weston-super-Mare make up the top ten of long British piers. All of them were originally built in the nineteenth century, for the purposes of walking an awfully long way out to sea and then back again.

7. Victorians were weird, weren't they?

8. Consider that this isn't actually the longest pier in the world, simply the longest pleasure pier. The overall top dog is the 4-mile-long shipping jetty at Progreso, Mexico. The biggest in the southern hemisphere is at Busselton, Western Australia, but if you fall in the water there, you may well get eaten by a shark.

9. If you still haven't reached the end yet, think up some stuff of your own to consider.

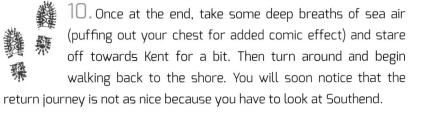

10. Once at the end, take some deep breaths of sea air (puffing out your chest for added comic effect) and stare off towards Kent for a bit. Then turn around and begin walking back to the shore. You will soon notice that the return journey is not as nice because you have to look at Southend.

11. Repeat, if you can be arsed.

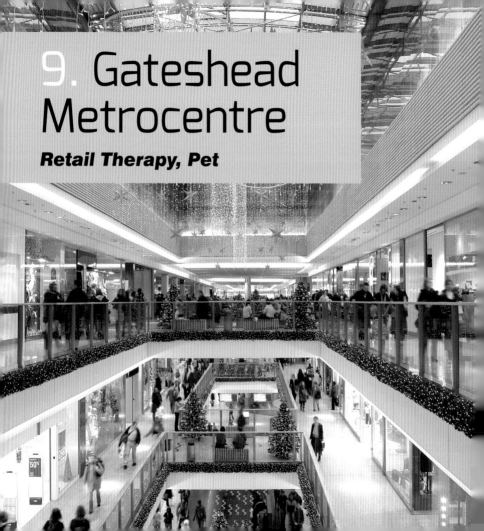

9. Gateshead Metrocentre

Retail Therapy, Pet

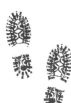

Thirty years ago, shopping in Britain still involved a certain amount of walking about in the fresh air. Then along came Metrocentre, a mega-mall built on the site of a former power station on the outskirts of Gateshead. It opened on 28 April 1986 (overshadowed somewhat by the announcement in Moscow of an explosion at a place called Chernobyl) and to this day remains the largest mall in Europe. This walk traces the steps of four intrepid adventurers, Robbie Scott, Lawrence Oates, Ed Wilson and 'Birdie' Bowers, who set out to reach a record store at the southern end of the mall while their wives and girlfriends were trying stuff on.

- **Difficulty** – *Like dragging a sledge laden with frozen seal blubber to the South Pole. And back again*
- **Useful items** – *A folding chair. Do you remember when they used to have chairs in Marks and Spencer so you could have a nice sit down?*
- **Likelihood of heroic yet ultimately futile self-sacrifice** – *I'm just going out now, chaps. I may be some time*

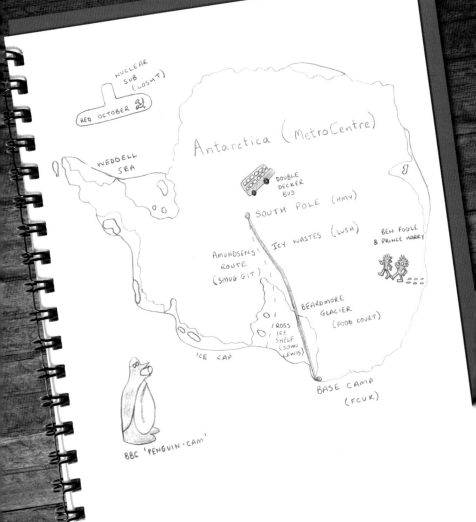

1.　Take the train to Metrocentre railway station (confusingly, National Rail variously describes the mall as metrocentre, MetroCentre and Metro Centre on its website, using all three variations on just one page. This is due to the inability to use English correctly which crossed the Atlantic at around the same time as shopping malls. Of course, if Chernobyl hadn't blown up and the West had lost the Cold War, inconsistent grammar would be the least of our worries). Take a deep breath of unfiltered oxygen because it is the last you are going to get for a while, then climb the stairs to the covered footbridge.

2.　The bridge will take you across to the bus terminal and then into the shopping centre itself, where you emerge at a branch of TK Maxx. You are now in the Blue sector, and there are four more sectors to explore (Red, Yellow, Green and Platinum), as well as three themed areas (the Village, the Forum and Qube). Metrocentre has around 340 shops occupying more than 2 million square feet of space – but it only scrapes into the world's top 50 largest malls. Top of the pile is New South China Mall in Dongguan, which has as an indoor rollercoaster, a replica Arc de Triomphe and a one-and-a-half-mile-long Venetian canal complete with gondolas.

3. This is where you pick up the trail of our explorers. In his diary, Scott notes: 'After 45 minutes waiting outside French Connection, Oates and I strike up a conversation with Bowers and Wilson, who are similarly indisposed. We agree to trek to the extreme south "pole" of the mall to look at some CDs in HMV [this is a historic document, remember]. Our provisions include a pound of pipe tobacco, a case of brandy, ten dozen petrel eggs and some ship's biscuits and we sally forth in high spirits.'

4. Walk along the upper level, avoiding the tide of shoppers – all of whom will appear to have lost the ability to nod or smile or acknowledge a fellow human being in any way. This is where Scott records: 'Our first camp has been an unmitigated disaster. Refused permission to build a fire to fry the eggs, we sought solace in brandy and a smoke – only to be informed those activities were in breach of health and safety regulations. Dined on cold biscuits. This is indeed a desolate, inhospitable place.'

5. Negotiate the 'food' court. The ambience is of end-of-term school dinner at a large and unruly comprehensive, while the cuisine on offer will often manage to be both artery-furring and unsatisfying. Scott records: 'As a change from ship's biscuits, we dined on some of the native food that is available here. My Chinese spare ribs were inedible, coated as they were in a gelatinous gloop, while Oates has tremendous heartburn after his triple burger and fries and Bowers has been strangely silent ever since his extra-extra hot peri peri chicken. At least the tent is warm tonight, if a trifle pungent.'

6. Continue beyond the cinema and return to the lower level of the shopping arcade. This is where the expedition began to run into serious trouble. 'Back to ship's biscuits. Wilson is beginning to suffer from snow blindness after staring too long at the strip lights, while I have blisters the size of dinner plates. At least HMV is within our grasp now, although my missus texted three times to ask where I was. I ignored her.'

7. Reach the southern end of the mall. Scott's diary states: 'Must fight the urge to sob uncontrollably. Arrive at the record store only to find that my boss, a cocky Norwegian sod called Amundsen, is already here, chatting with an attractive female sales assistant about the latest indie music and trying on trendy headphones. All is lost. I cannot go in and listen to any more of his crap. Inform my companions that we must return to base. Each of them agrees readily enough, and I suspect I am not the only one to have had a text from the wife.'

8. Return to the start of your walk. Scott's final entry was made somewhere between Lush and Hollister. 'Damn this place, damn it all to hell. We ate the last of our biscuits this morning. Some hours later, Oates announced that he was going out for a walk. He has not returned. I can feel my strength ebbing away. I would succumb to oblivion but I don't altogether like the hungry way that Bowers is eyeing me up...'

8. Cape Wrath Bombing Range

Is That a Puffin or a... KA-BOOM!

Cape Wrath is the most north-westerly point of the British mainland, home only to a lighthouse and cafe on the cliffs, and surrounded by 80 square miles of uninhabited moorland known locally as the Parph. This wild landscape is owned by the Ministry of Defence, which uses Cape Wrath as Europe's largest bombing range. It is the only place in Europe where 1,000-pound bombs can be tested, and frequently hosts large NATO training exercises, when the range is shelled by navy vessels offshore and strafed by fighter jets. Fancy a stroll?

- **Difficulty** – *Boot camp in* Full Metal Jacket
- **Useful items** – *Warm socks, sturdy boots, body armour, replacement blood/plasma kit*
- **Likelihood of a military cover-up in the event of your death** – *Prepare to become another Internet conspiracy theory*

1.   Drive to Durness in Sutherland. It's a long way and it will take you around seven hours to get there... from Glasgow. From anywhere south of Milton Keynes it's going to take you more like 13–15 hours, without stopping, and to remove any possibility of enjoyment you should aim to complete the last six hours through the magnificent scenery of the Highlands in complete darkness.

2.   Timing is crucial to this walk, and you should wait until the day before the bombing range is to be closed for a military training exercise. The MoD describes this area as 'the last great wilderness' and yet at the same time is perfectly happy to routinely pepper it with live ordnance. Local opinion is divided on the bombing, although people on both sides of the debate have become dab hands at catching falling crockery as the shockwaves rattle their homes. Park at Keoldale, head south on the A838, and wait for the ferry across the loch to the Kyle of Durness.

3. From the ferry landing there is an 11-mile single-track road leading to the lighthouse. The cape is regularly blasted by icy 120-mile-per-hour winds and the track is notoriously treacherous and steep in places. Even when it is not coming under fire from Her Majesty's armed forces, the cape can be cut off for weeks at a time due to bad weather. Tell the ferry operator that you do not require a return journey, as you intend to hike out across the Parph to Sandwood Bay.

4. Once you are beyond the first military sentry point at the entrance to the bombing range, strike out across the bog and find somewhere to bivvy down for the night. You can while away the hours by birdwatching, as the area is home to tens of thousands of seabirds – which seem to thrive despite the occasional danger of being blown to smithereens. (Who knows, they may actually enjoy the diversion? After all, life must be pretty dull at times for a guillemot.)

5. At first light, return to the track and resume your journey to the lighthouse, which was built by Robert Stevenson (the *Treasure Island* author's old man). The thrill of seeing Britain's highest sea cliffs at Clo Moor and the enormous feeling of isolation will be tempered somewhat by the RAF Typhoons screaming in overhead. There might even be a US Navy carrier group shelling the range from a mile or two offshore. If you come across a brightly painted target, move on rapidly or you are liable to end up as pink mist.

6. It might be worth remembering that a 1,000-pound bomb will blow a crater in the ground up to 30 feet deep and has a blast radius of around 300 yards. Yikes! Pick up the pace, only a few more miles to go now!

7. The chances are you will be picked up by a military patrol before you reach The Ozone Café at the lighthouse for a nice, relaxing pot of tea and a slice of cake. The soldiers might be somewhat irate after having to call a halt to a training exercise costing several hundreds of thousands of pounds, but at least you will get to have a ride in the back of an army Land Rover.

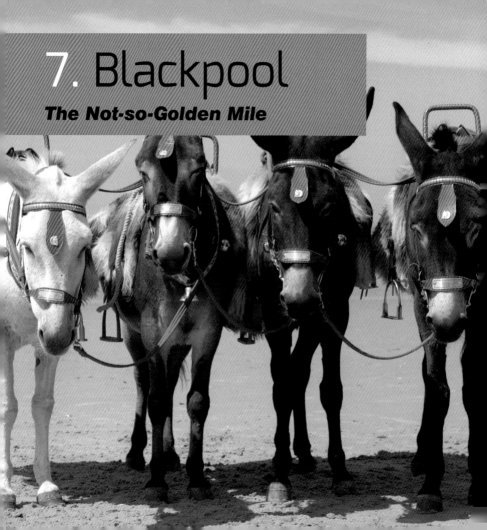

7. Blackpool
The Not-so-Golden Mile

You are now about to embark on a drunken odyssey through a seaside town with more holiday beds than Greece. For maximum mind-altering effect, you should try the walk on a bank holiday weekend when the resort is heaving with rowdy stag and hen parties, day-tripping football hooligans and assorted binge drinkers from across Britain. As an added bonus, you can also take in three of England's ten most deprived areas – a bit like the 'Three Peaks Challenge', but with more heroin.

- **Difficulty** – *Pint of Stella, in one*
- **Useful items** – *Torch, spare batteries, 40 Regal King Size, condoms*
- **Likelihood of being beaten up, falling in the sea, vomiting in the street or catching a stubborn venereal disease** – *A racing certainty*

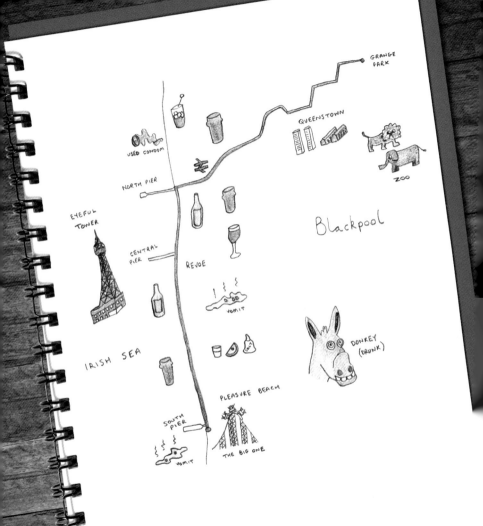

GRANGE PARK

QUEENSTOWN

ZOO

USED CONDOM

NORTH PIER

Blackpool

EYEFUL TOWER

CENTRAL PIER

REVOE

VOMIT

DONKEY (DRUNK)

IRISH SEA

PLEASURE BEACH

SOUTH PIER

THE BIG ONE

VOMIT

 1. Begin your walk in Grange Park, a sprawling council estate just off the A587 on the eastern outskirts of town. Say goodbye to your car at the shops on Chepstow Road.

 2. Head west, towards the sea, through a rabbit warren of terraced streets and high-rise blocks. This is Queenstown, an entry in the national deprivation top ten but a remarkably friendly place, nevertheless.

 3. Walk along Talbot Road to the railway station, in the heart of Blackpool's red-light district. Several nearby fast-food premises were linked to a grooming ring involving underage runaways and the unsolved disappearances of two schoolgirls, although murder charges against the men who allegedly joked that they had 'gone into the kebabs' were dropped. Bon appétit!

4. Arrive at the promenade by the North Pier and take a deep breath of sea air. Back in the 1930s, this bone-chilling sou'westerly breeze was a major selling point for the 'Lung of Lancashire' and led indirectly to the introduction of paid holidays as a universal right. However, this isn't *The Road to Wigan Pier* so there is no need to get all 'Orwell-ed up' about workers' rights in smoky mill towns; this is Blackpool in the 2010s and you are here to get pissed. Choose a nearby pub (there are several) and start drinking.

5. After several beverages of your choice, you should be sufficiently inebriated to enter the Tower Lounge, located at the base of the famous rusty phallic totem that lurks in the low grey clouds above the town. The lounge itself is a cavernous, sticky-floored den of iniquity frequented by marauding gangs of inebriated Yorkshiremen and hen parties from South Wales singing along to 'Angels' by Robbie Williams. They may seem friendly now but come 2 a.m. they will be trying to fight you or shag you – or quite possibly both at the same time.

6. Continue unsteadily along the prom, stopping at one of the many outlets of overpriced tourist tat. Try to buy at least one of the following: a baseball cap with a plastic turd on the brim; a lurid red boiled sweet in the shape of male genitalia; a bottle of 'poppers', or amyl nitrate; a T-shirt with a xenophobic/sexist/offensive slogan or image, such as Wile E. Coyote humping a startled Road Runner and declaring, 'Beep beep now, you bastard'; plastic breasts; a pile of rubber sick.

7. Next, drop into one of the slot arcades, such as Mr B's or Coral Island, to jostle with the teenagers too young to get served in the pubs and high from the aforementioned poppers. Spend £1, £2 or even £3 a time to shoot zombies, race a motorbike or beat the living daylights out of some deformed martial arts oddity, before joining the old-age pensioners trying to win a life-sized stuffed tiger or a big box of Maltesers on the bingo.

8. You might now be in danger of sobering up, so resume your ramble along the prom in a southerly direction. Pubs include the nautical-themed Flagship (the theme possibly being rum, sodomy and the lash), The Jaggy Thistle, a Scottish bar that offers a wee slice of grinding Glaswegian misery, or Yates's Wine Lodge, a favourite meeting place for pre-arranged soccer violence. If possible, take a short diversion inland to Revoe, a sand-blasted seaside favela that completes your deprivation hat-trick.

9. Continue, as best you can, towards the Pleasure Beach, where you round off the day by going on The Big One roller coaster again and again until you throw up spectacularly into a litter bin, while horrified parents cover their children's eyes at the disgusting spectacle. Don't bother going back for the car, it's probably halfway to Liverpool by now.

6. Sellafield

Apocalypse Nowt

In one of England's forgotten corners, squeezed between the Cumbrian Mountains and the murky Irish Sea, this walk allows you to admire the unfolding vista of cooling towers, steel chimneys, mothballed reactors and crumbling concrete bunkers. This is the Sellafield reprocessing plant, where much of the world's nuclear waste is turned into uranium, plutonium and a kind of toxic sludge that will still be deadly in several hundred thousand years' time. Britain has been described as the planet's 'nuclear dustbin', and you are about to step on the pedal and peer under the lid.

- **Difficulty** – *Not exactly splitting the atom*
- **Useful items** – *Sunscreen, a bottle of water, Geiger counter*
- **Likelihood of Westminster ever building a nuclear waste reprocessing plant in the south of England** – *Big fat zero*

1. Park at South Parade in Seascale and walk north along the beach, joining the Cumbrian Coastal Way. This quiet village inspired Victorian author George Gissing to write his novel *The Odd Women*, and after meeting some of the locals you might conclude that his title is still accurate throughout much of West Cumbria today.

2. Cross the River Calder on BNFL Bridge; as the river flows through the middle of the plant, do NOT be tempted to stop for a paddle. You may, however, pause to admire Building B30, a rain-stained concrete box once described by Sellafield Deputy Managing Director George Beveridge as 'the most hazardous industrial building in Western Europe'. The second most hazardous, B31, is right next door. Many of the warehouses before you, according to one eloquent but unnamed engineer quoted in *The Guardian*, contain an unverifiable quantity of 'appalling radioactive crap'. Most of it is our legacy of the quest for an atomic bomb in the 1950s and the merry, possibly LSD-induced recklessness of the 1960s when spent nuclear fuel rods were simply chucked into what appears to be a series of indoor swimming pools. The preferred modern method is to bury the stuff far, far, far underground and wait until *Homo sapiens* have either become extinct or evolved into an entirely different species altogether.

3. Leave the coastal path at Sellafield railway station and turn inland, following the road along the northern boundary of the plant. At this point you may attract the attention of the Special Branch detectives charged with keeping an eye on the site – and with between 50 and 100 tons of weapons-grade plutonium stockpiled here at any one time, they can perhaps be forgiven for being a trifle twitchy. To avoid the inconvenience of two weeks' detention without charge, as well as being labelled a 'terror suspect' in the newspapers, this walk is probably not advisable if you are of Arabic or South Asian origin or have a sense of humour which might compel you to joke that you are here on a 'recce for al-Qaeda'.

4. At the roundabout, turn right and walk past the former visitors' centre car park. Incredibly, Sellafield was once the most popular tourist attraction in West Cumbria and children on school trips, science geeks and disgruntled holidaymakers were given a clip-on name badge and taken on a rambling, largely security-free walking tour of a facility that stores enough explosive material to destroy civilisation. The tours ended after 9/11 and the visitors' centre is now a somewhat underused conference facility.

5. Walk up the hill past the Sella Park Country House Hotel, a sixteenth-century manor house and possibly one of the most unlikely wedding venues in Britain. Once you crest the rise and emerge from the trees of Knockinghill Wood, you immediately enter the hamlet of Calder Bridge. Follow the busy A595, before turning off again towards Seascale Hall. This path will take you along Sellafield's southern boundary, and if you time the walk correctly, it will appear to glow orange as the sun sets over the western horizon. This can be *most* disconcerting.

6. Beyond the hall, take a short detour from the footpath to an ancient circle of standing stones. The ten Bronze Age megaliths, some standing 6 feet tall, were unearthed in 1949 by a party of local schoolboys and their teacher. As you complete the walk into Seascale, try not to imagine what might be dug up around here in the year 4000.

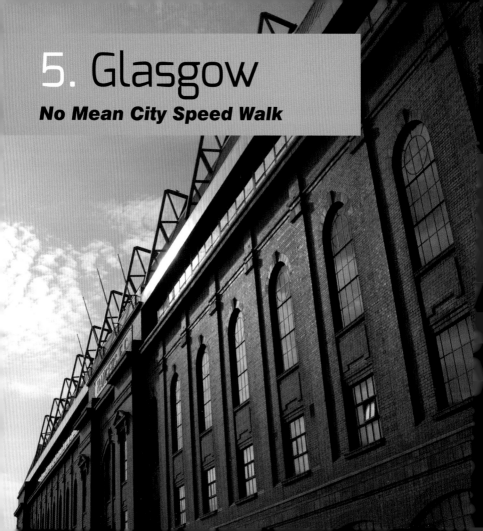

5. Glasgow

No Mean City Speed Walk

Glasgow is a great city, inhabited in the most part by warm, welcoming and funny people. Forget the old jibes about deep-fried Mars bars, razor gangs and depressing rain (actually, that last one is true); Glasgow is now the haunt of foodies, fashionistas and film stars. However, on certain days, when the city's Rangers and Celtic football teams are playing each other, the atmosphere can get a little, ahem, tense. For a truly great fitness work out, try this on Old Firm day.

- **Difficulty** – *A Teddy Bears' picnic*
- **Useful items** – *Warm clothing, sense of humour, deep historical and religious grievance*
- **Likelihood of severe physical harm** – *You're gonnae get your fuckin' head kicked in… unless you are fit enough to outrun a horde of Glaswegians… Oh, hang on a minute*

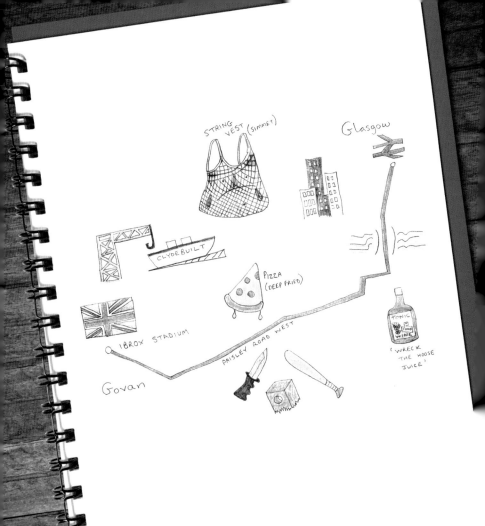

STRING VEST (SIMMET)

Glasgow

CLYDEBUILT

PIZZA (DEEP FRIED)

IBROX STADIUM

PAISLEY ROAD WEST

Govan

TONIC WINE

'WRECK THE HOOSE JUICE'

1. For ideal speed-walking conditions, choose a day when Rangers are playing at home. Travel to Govan before the game on the Glasgow Subway – known as the Clockwork Orange and equipped with tiny, tangerine-hued trains that would not look out of place in a Thomas the Tank Engine play set. Rangers supporters like to enliven the journey by 'doing the bouncy', which involves hurling themselves up and down en masse until the miniscule carriages begin to shake violently.

2. Alight at Ibrox subway station and walk down Copland Road to Edmiston Drive. The club helpfully advises that the stadium is located at Number 150, although most people should be able to find it without the aid of a full postal address, as it looms over this part of Glasgow like Sauron's Tower from *The Lord of the Rings*. In keeping with the theme of fantasy villains, Ibrox is known throughout Scottish football as 'Castle Grayskull'.

3. For the uninitiated, Rangers is traditionally a Protestant club while Celtic is Roman Catholic. Many supporters also align themselves to one side or other of the historic Loyalist/ Republican divide in Northern Ireland – as if one nation's quota of religious hatred wasn't enough to be getting on with.

4. The area will be busy with fast-food vans and you could grab a snack while you wait for the match to finish. Enjoy your hot dog but don't be tempted to eat too much, as you are going to have to be in good shape for the next bit.

5. Shortly after the final whistle, as 45,000 pumped-up supporters are spilling out onto the streets, remove your jacket to reveal the famous green and white hoops of the Celtic home jersey, wrap an Irish tricolor around your shoulders and perhaps pull on a novelty Guinness hat. Then begin to sing, at the top of your voice, the Parkhead anthem and IRA tribute song 'The Boys of the Old Brigade'. This works particularly well if Rangers have just lost.

6. Still singing, begin to 'speed walk' along Edmiston Drive towards the city centre. You may even decide it is advisable to break into a hasty trot or even a full-blown run at this point, although you should avoid a desperate life-or-death sprint as you still have around three and a half miles to go.

7. Turn onto Paisley Road West and rapidly make your way east through the Kinning Park district. There are some Celtic-friendly pubs around here but the regulars will probably not thank you for bringing a baying and bloodthirsty mob to their front door. Continue on past the Springfield Quay cinema/bingo/bowling complex and under the M8 flyover into Tradeston.

8. Follow West Street to the banks of the River Clyde. You now have two options. Either a) cross the Commerce Street bridge and follow Oswald Street north to Central Station, before boarding a train to... well, anywhere really, or b) jump into the water yourself, thus saving your exhausted pursuers the trouble of throwing you in.

9. For variety, you can have a similar experience by donning a Rangers shirt and heading on over to Celtic Park, located at 18 Kerrydale Street in Parkhead, a delightful district known for its bijou wine bars and avant-garde street theatre. After the match, when you reveal your light blue colours, Union Jack and perhaps attempt a verse or two of the bigoted old Rangers standard, 'Hullo, hullo, we are the Billy Boys', your escape route will take you west along London Road into the city centre. Alternatively, you can try the Hampden speed walk (wearing an England shirt after a Scotland match) or the Tory speed walk (wearing a Conservative rosette and an 'I Love Maggie Thatcher' T-shirt, which works from just about anywhere in Glasgow).

4. Wallingford
A Midsomer Night's Scream

Wallingford was once one of the largest towns in England, part of Alfred the Great's defensive line protecting Wessex from the bloodthirsty Viking hordes. Ironically, considering the effort that went into keeping its residents safe, the town now thrives on a reputation as the homicide capital of Middle England, if not the world. The TV show *Midsomer Murders* has been filmed here since 1997 and the body count is now rapidly approaching 250. Honduras is supposedly the most deadly country on earth, with a murder rate of 82 per 100,000; in Midsomer, it is around 3,850 per 100,000.

- *Difficulty – More dangerous than a hike through the Columbian coca fields*
- *Useful items – Chocolate bar, banana, flimsy alibi for Sunday night when Lady D'Izzi was beaten to death with a bag of frozen peas*
- *Likelihood of being murdered by an eccentric serial killer – Exceedingly high*

1. Start your walk at Wallingford's market square, which will be recognisable to slack-jawed Sunday-night television viewers as the centre of the fictional town of Causton. It surely can't be a coincidence that the bloody killing spree began when John Nettles arrived to take up a CID job in rural Oxfordshire, having failed to prevent a similar crimewave in Jersey in the 1980s. Despite his twinkly-eyed charm and remarkable clear-up record (solving most cases in two hours, including ad breaks) the man is a walking murder magnet.

2. Walk south, along St Mary's Street, to the Corn Exchange Theatre, possibly the world's most dangerous arts venue. Go inside to catch the end of a play by an extremely ropey am-dram group, which will end in geysers of gore spurting from a severed jugular when the lead actress has her throat slit with a prop razor live on stage (the devious killer having earlier removed the safety tape from the blade). The theatre has also been connected to 16 other slayings, including an au pair who was injected with liquid nicotine (all murders in Wallingford are achingly middle class).

3. Exit the theatre before the police arrive (you probably won't be interviewed anyway, unless you are a disgruntled gardener at loggerheads with an aristocratic local family). Continue along St Mary's Street, which becomes Reading Road and eventually takes you out of Wallingford altogether. As you leave town, you will probably bump into a wealthy, gin-soaked and still remarkably attractive widow and quickly discover that you have a shared interest in some unlikely topic – erotic cake decorations, for example. In all likelihood, she will then invite you to lunch at the manor house.

4. Arrive at the manor house on the outskirts of Cholsey. Lunch will be a fraught affair, undershot by family tension, meaningful glances and repressed sexual urges, and will end with somebody either choking to death on a poisoned cucumber sandwich or being chopped in two by an axe held aloft by an apparently empty suit of armour. After being present at the scene of two murders, you will probably be interviewed – briefly, without a recording being taken – by the local plod. Incidentally, John Nettles has now been replaced by Neil Dudgeon, who has previously worked alongside such law enforcement legends as DI Jack Frost, Inspector Morse and Sherlock Holmes. Perhaps as a result of this impressive CV, he's never failed to solve a case yet either.

5. Arrive, somewhat breathlessly, at the medieval centre of Cholsey (fittingly, the queen of fictional crime Agatha Christie is buried in the village) and take Ilges Lane and then a public footpath across the fields to the former Fair Mile Hospital, now an executive housing development. As you pass by, a smarmy developer will be struck over the head with a 'For Sale' sign and tumble from a balcony to his death, landing at your feet. Wait patiently for the police to arrive, while everybody acts as though three murders in one afternoon in a pleasant corner of rural England is really not that unusual.

6. Continue south on Reading Road towards Moulsford. If you are black or Asian, you will probably avoid being murdered or even involved in the plot in any way (producer Brian True-May was suspended after describing the show as 'the last bastion of Englishness' because it never featured ethnic minorities). Follow the footpath along the riverbank, where you will discover the body of a local champion rower slumped in his boat with an oar embedded in his skull. He was previously the prime suspect for the murders and the spotlight will now inevitably turn on you. Nevertheless, you should be free to continue your walk (few people are remanded in custody in Midsomer, as that would reduce the number of gorgeous location shots).

7. Continue on to Goring-on-Thames, stepping over the bodies of a cricket club stalwart battered to death with his bat, a busybody villager shot with an antique crossbow and the flirtatious wife of a stressed-out stockbroker strangled with her own pantyhose and left sprawled in a bramble bush. Enjoy a pint and a pork pie in the pub, because if you try to run you will surely be arrested and charged with multiple counts of premeditated, first-degree murder.

8. Neil Dudgeon and his handsome yet dim-witted companion, possibly joined by the resident pathologist who appears to take an unusually active role in such investigations, will arrive at the pub, where all the suspects (including you) are conveniently gathered. In classic whodunnit fashion, the inspector will then point the finger of suspicion at everybody present, before revealing that it was... the vicar, who had been enjoying a torrid affair with the wealthy widow. In order to keep it secret, he decided to bump off a significant number of his parishioners for increasingly ludicrous motives.

9. While the vicar is clapped in handcuffs and dragged away, voicing his feeble protestations, you are now free to enjoy a convivial drink with the surviving members of the local aristocratic family and the various grieving widows and children, all of whom will have taken the appalling slaughter of their loved ones with remarkable equanimity. Don't hang around, though, as there will be another six or seven people murdered the following Sunday.

3. Skegness
Nasty Smells in Stinkamells

Skegness in Lincolnshire was founded by a Dane named Skeggi (meaning 'the bearded one') and the hairy old rascal would no doubt appreciate that he is remembered still in the town's nickname. Today, Skeggi is probably best known for the giant Butlin's holiday resort that lies just beyond its northern boundary, near the villages of Ingoldmells and Addlethorpe. Located between these three near neighbours is a sewage works that has been described as the smelliest in Britain, which will give this walk a truly unforgettable flavour.

- **Difficulty** – *Depends which way the wind is blowing*
- **Useful items** – *A flask of hot coffee, a clothes peg, smelling salts*
- **Likelihood of the stench being so bad it makes your eyes bleed and your hair turn green and your nose go inverted** – *Don't get carried away, it's only poo*

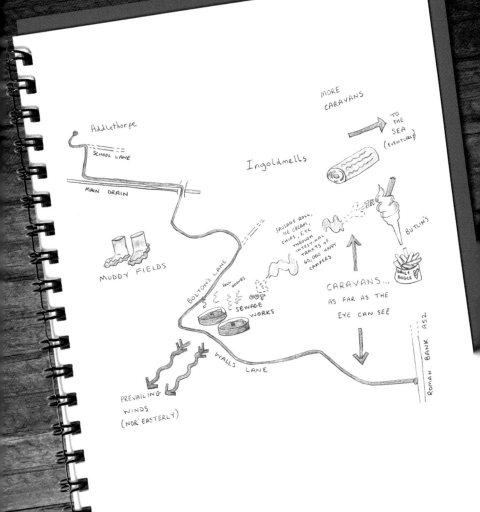

1. Start in Addlethorpe, on Church Lane. The village features in the Domesday Book, the largest of 25 muddy settlements in the ancient 'Wapentake of Candleshoe'. Today, more than 900 years after the tight-assed Normans visited with their quills and their parchment and their French superiority complex, it still has a similar number of residents, while Skeggi – which was so insignificant in the eleventh century that it was not even recorded – has mushroomed in size and is now famous for its bracing air. Take a deep sniff as you walk down School Lane. Lovely.

2. Take the first turning on your right onto a footpath through the flat fields. For added unpleasantness, you should aim to walk during the summer and preferably after a few days of intense rainfall. This will ensure that the heavy clay soil will stick to your boots like cement and weigh you down with every step. When you reach the drainage channel, turn east and walk along the footpath towards the sea. Your nostrils may just be able to pick up the first hint of something unpleasant...

3.   Ingoldmells, the neighbouring village to Addlethorpe, is by far the larger of the two, with around 2,000 permanent residents – and during the school holidays the population swells to around 10 or even 20 times that number. Billy Butlins opened Britain's first holiday camp here in 1936 and the fields between Ingoldmells and Skegness are now packed with thousands upon thousands of static caravans. Unfortunately, the Anglian Water waste treatment plant on Bolton's Lane cannot always cope with the cascading end results of all those ice creams, bags of chips and pints of lager.

4.   Continue along the edge of the drainage channel until you come to a single-track road bridge leading to a small farm. Go across the bridge and strike out on the footpath leading south-east through the muddy fields. Your boots should now weigh roughly as much as two large bags of sand; if you were the intended victim of a Mafia hit, the goons would not even have to weigh you down before tipping you over the edge of the harbour. However, as you approach the sewage works, you will probably wish that you really were swimming with da fishes. Arrive on Bolton's Lane and turn right.

5. Residents of Ingoldmells have been complaining about the foul reek from the sewage works for at least a decade, and in spite of efforts by Anglian Water, the problem has persisted. One guesthouse owner told a local newspaper that a holidaymaker had suggested the village be renamed 'Stinkamells', adding: 'On a nice day, if the smell comes you have to close your windows and if you have washing on the line it smells of it.' If you observe carefully, you will see the ruts in the fields showing the mass exodus of caravans – the ones that were able to get away – at the height of the annual summer aroma. Walk south on Bolton's Lane, if you can stand it, and arrive at the sewage plant.

6. Turn east onto Wall's Lane, skirting the southern boundary of the plant. You are now just a few hundred yards from the healthy ozone of the North Sea, but it may not be the salt tang that is bringing tears to your eyes. The sewage outflow from the plant is a distant 1.5 kilometres out to sea and the Environment Agency says the bathing water quality at Ingoldmells is good. Pause here to contemplate the report that says the situation has 'improved substantially since the 1980s'. Not much consolation for those of us who used to come here on holiday as kids, then.

7.   Walk down Wall's Lane through the vast hinterland of static caravans, ranged on the flat plain like unwieldy PVC buffalo, until you reach the main A52, known as Roman Bank because it runs arrow-straight along the coast. Call in for a well-deserved snifter or three at Cheers Bar, then take a deep breath and retrace your steps.

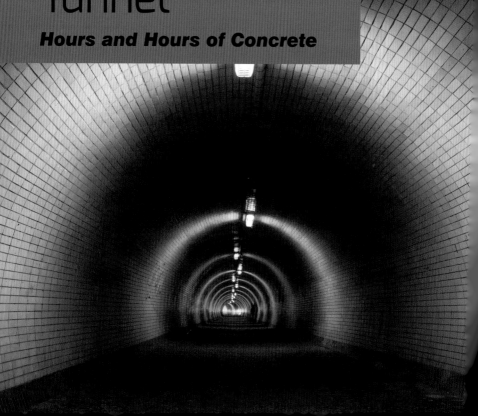

2. Channel Tunnel

Hours and Hours of Concrete

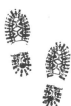

The British are an island race. Shakespeare described his homeland as a 'precious stone set in the silver sea' and Churchill vowed that 'we shall defend our island whatever the cost'. We like living in splendid, stormy isolation, thumbing our noses at Europe. And yet on 6 May 1994, when the Eurotunnel was officially opened by the Queen, Britain became an island that you can walk to. Arguably, using some admittedly twisted logic, we are now a *tied island* – one that is attached to a larger land mass by a thin spit of sand – and this walk will prove it.

- **Difficulty** – *Très stupid*
- **Useful items** – *Walker's headlamp, French dictionary, passport*
- **Likelihood of bumping into an incoming stampede of benefit-scrounging asylum seekers** – *Depends what paper you read*

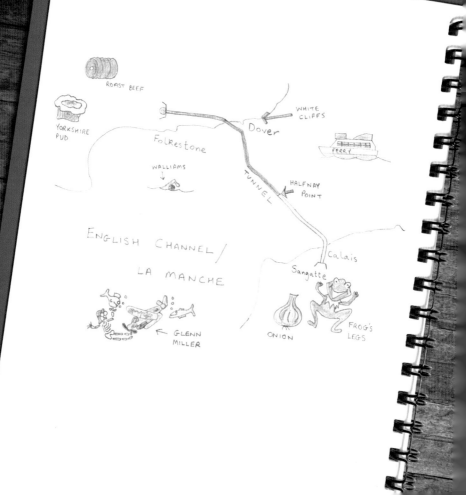

1. Start at the Eurotunnel Rail Control Centre at Cheriton, just north of Folkestone. This is the big building near to where the tunnel dives beneath the bulk of Castle Hill. Incidentally, this walk is only for the truly committed as you will either have to a) bribe an employee to lend you their security pass, b) develop a James Bond-like ability to sneak into places or c) actually get a job with Eurotunnel. From the control centre, you will be able to access the entrance to the service tunnel that runs between the twin rail tunnels all the way to France.

2. This brightly lit subterranean slipway is about 15 feet in diameter. There are rounded, concrete walls painted with all manner of confusing symbols and two narrow vehicle lanes beneath your feet, while overhead air-conditioning ducts, water pipes and electrical cables carrying 50,000 volts all hum loudly and annoyingly. Get used to this view, because this is all that you are going to be seeing for a good long while. Begin walking along the tunnel.

3. You might notice cables embedded in the concrete floor – these are used to guide the service tunnel transport system vehicles, including maintenance trucks, ambulances and fire engines. These rubber-wheeled babies can zip along at 50 miles per hour, so be prepared to jump out of the way at a moment's notice.

4. It is 6 miles below ground before you even leave British soil, as the concrete tunnel weaves its way eastward along the south coast to Shakespeare Cliff, which is where you will turn south and begin to delve beneath the English Channel.

5. The monotony of the scenery will be relieved (but only slightly) by the cross-passages every 375 metres, connecting the service tunnel to the two rail tunnels. These are used for maintenance or as escape routes in the event of an emergency. You could try counting them to make the walk more interesting. Alternatively, if you have a walking companion, try a game of 'I spy'. ('I spy, with my little eye, something beginning with C.' 'Is it concrete?' 'Yes.')

6. You are going deeper and ever deeper underground, down to more than 75 metres below the seabed. The horrible, pressing sensation of claustrophobia will be unmistakable to anybody who has ever travelled on a rush-hour train in London. From time to time, the overhead lights will be switched off, leaving you in complete darkness. What is that dripping noise you can hear? Who truly knows what manner of things lurk down here in the bowels of the earth? In fact, the service vehicles are not the only things you have to watch out for. In November 2012, a journalist from *Top Gear* magazine drove a battery-powered car along the service tunnel to France, so as if things weren't already bad enough, you also run the risk of being mown down by Jeremy Clarkson.

7. At the halfway stage, you will pass the point where Englishman Graham Fagg and Frenchman Phillippe Cozette broke through to join the two ends of the service tunnel on 30 October 1990. It is marked by a sign reading 'Mid Point', the only landmark of the entire journey, so you should consider stopping for a photo.

8. From here on, the tunnel begins to climb again towards Calais and the workman's graffiti daubed on the walls is all in French. Technically, of course, you are now in France and therefore out of the jurisdiction of *Britain's Worst Walks*. So, rather than achieving the notable feat of actually walking to Europe, you must now turn around and retrace your steps to Folkestone. Chin up, chest out; remember, you're British. Ooh, look, there's some more concrete.

1. City of London

What a Bunch of Bankers

In 2008, one group of people brought the world economy crashing to its knees. They had been taking other people's money, in the form of their mortgages and life savings, and gambling with it, just as though they were in a colossal, imaginary and entirely consequence-free casino. These people were bankers, and by and large most of them were not punished. In fact, many were rewarded with massive bonuses and allowed to continue fixing interest rates and mis-selling products. Most of them live and work around here. For this, Britain's worst walk, we have recruited a spirit guide – one of London's most famous ever residents – to lead you in his bloodstained footprints.

- **Difficulty** – 'Greed is good' was supposed to be ironic, you fuckers
- **Useful items** – GPS system, top hat, cape and walking cane, detailed anatomical knowledge
- **Likelihood of being gripped by all-consuming rage** – High

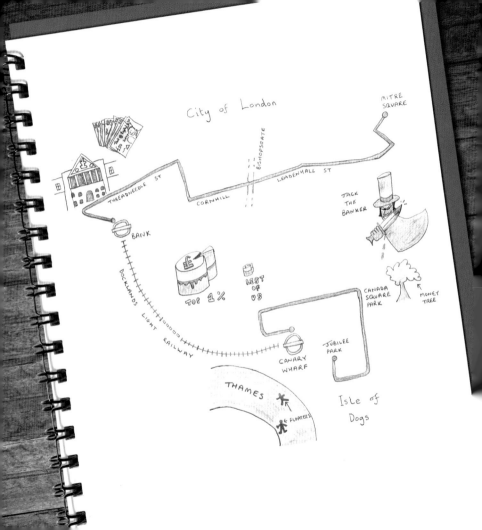

1. Good afternoon, ladies and gentlemen, my name is... well, I'd rather not give you my real name, but history knows me as Jack the Ripper. For more than a century I was the most detested and reviled figure in the long and sordid history of London. And then along came the credit crunch and the dawning realisation that the entire country was being royally shafted by the financiers and bond traders and investment bankers who infest my old stomping ground. These fiscally dyslexic arse weevils gleefully describe themselves as 'Masters of the Universe' and think nothing of rewarding their collective failure with 'bonuses' totalling millions of pounds per annum, while thousands of families across the land go hungry as a direct result of their actions. And people still think that I'm a villain!

2. Start your walk in Mitre Square. This is where they found my fourth victim, Kate Eddowes. It was a dark, smog-filled place in those days, even when the sun was overhead, cast into shadow by a tea warehouse. Today it is overlooked by some peculiar-looking glass edifices, including one that resembles a gherkin and another that is the home of Lloyds TSB, a bank that had to be 'bailed out' by the taxpayer, whatever that means.

3. Walk west along Leadenhall Street into the City. The streets will be thronged with smartly dressed financial workers, spending their filthy lucre on ludicrously overpriced sandwiches (£5 for a rocket and crayfish wrap? In my day, oysters were three for a penny) and sparkling water, which is full of dangerous-sounding minerals (we had lead and cholera in ours, free of charge).

4. Cross Bishopsgate, within sight of the London headquarters of the Royal Bank of Scotland. This also had to be rescued by the public, after an avaricious Scotchman named Fred Goodwin led the bank – and with it, the nation – to within inches of the abyss. To the south is Barclays Bank, where another chief executive – a Yankee named 'Bonus' Bob Diamond – received a £2.7 million sum upon stepping down from his post in disgrace. The *Concise Oxford English Dictionary* defines bonus as 'a sum of money added to a person's wages for good performance'. I confess that even I do not understand the perfidious ways of the modern world.

5. Walk down Cornhill and skirt the Royal Exchange to emerge on Threadneedle Street. Go south past the Bank of England to Bank station and board the Docklands Light Railway. These trains are famous for not having anybody at the wheel, a bit like the British economy, it seems to me. The line takes you within sight of Berner Street, where they found my third victim, Elizabeth 'Long Liz' Stride. Aptly enough, it is close to a large office building that for many years was home to NatWest and then the Royal Bank of Scotland. I once saw Fred 'the Shred' Goodwin here, furiously berating a member of staff over some trifling indiscretion, and I knew right away that I liked the cut of his jib. Even down to the nickname.

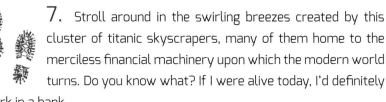

6. Alight at Canary Wharf in the heart of the Docklands financial district. We are now a little too far east for my liking, in what was once the Empire's thriving commercial underbelly, teeming with jack tars and vagabonds from every country on earth and all manner of undesirable ruffians from each corner of Britain. Now I come to think of it, it has not changed all that much since 1888. At least there will be no anti-capitalist protestors around, as these malodorous individuals were indefinitely banned from the whole of Canary Wharf in 2011 in case they should exercise their right to free speech and stage some kind of protest.

7. Stroll around in the swirling breezes created by this cluster of titanic skyscrapers, many of them home to the merciless financial machinery upon which the modern world turns. Do you know what? If I were alive today, I'd definitely work in a bank…

Have you enjoyed this book?
If so, why not write a review on your favourite website?

If you're interested in finding out more about our books,
find us on Facebook at **Summersdale Publishers**
and follow us on Twitter at **@Summersdale**.

Thanks very much for buying this Summersdale book.

www.summersdale.com